YORK NOTES

# Children
# of the Dust

Louise Lawrence

Notes by Catherine Allison

 Longman      York Press

YORK PRESS
322 Old Brompton Road, London SW5 9JH

ADDISON WESLEY LONGMAN LIMITED
Edinburgh Gate, Harlow,
Essex CM20 2JE, United Kingdom
Associated companies, branches and representatives throughout the world

First published 1998

ISBN 0–582–36822–7

Designed by Vicki Pacey, Trojan Horse, London
Illustrated by Jonathan Edwards
Family tree by Vicki Pacey, Trojan Horse, London
Phototypeset by Gem Graphics, Trenance, Mawgan Porth, Cornwall
Colour reproduction and film output by Spectrum Colour
Produced by Addison Wesley Longman China Limited, Hong Kong

# CONTENTS

# PREFACE

York Notes are designed to give you a broader perspective on works of literature studied at GCSE and equivalent levels. We have carried out extensive research into the needs of the modern literature student prior to publishing this new edition. Our research showed that no existing series fully met students' requirements. Rather than present a single authoritative approach, we have provided alternative viewpoints, empowering students to reach their own interpretations of the text. York Notes provide a close examination of the work and include biographical and historical background, summaries, glossaries, analyses of characters, themes, structure and language, cultural connections and literary terms.

If you look at the Contents page you will see the structure for the series. However, there's no need to read from the beginning to the end as you would with a novel, play, poem or short story. Use the Notes in the way that suits you. Our aim is to help you with your understanding of the work, not to dictate how you should learn.

York Notes are written by English teachers and examiners, with an expert knowledge of the subject. They show you how to succeed in coursework and examination assignments, guiding you through the text and offering practical advice. Questions and comments will extend, test and reinforce your knowledge. Attractive colour design and illustrations improve clarity and understanding, making these Notes easy to use and handy for quick reference.

York Notes are ideal for:
- Essay writing
- Exam preparation
- Class discussion

The author of these Notes is Catherine Allison, a full-time Head of English in a secondary school in the South East of England. She has a Master's degree in English and is Senior Examiner for English Literature for a major GCS 'A' Examination Board.

The text used in these Notes is the Red Fox edition, published by Random House in 1995.

*Health Warning:* **This study guide will enhance your understanding, but should not replace the reading of the original text and/or study in class.**

# PART ONE

# INTRODUCTION

## HOW TO STUDY A NOVEL

You have bought this book because you wanted to study a novel on your own. This may supplement classwork.

- You will need to read the novel several times. Start by reading it quickly for pleasure, then read it slowly and carefully. Further readings will generate new ideas and help you to memorise the details of the story.
- Make careful notes on themes, plot and characters of the novel. The plot will change some of the characters. Who changes?
- The novel may not present events chronologically. Does the novel you are reading begin at the beginning of the story or does it contain flashbacks and a muddled time sequence? Can you think why?
- How is the story told? Is it narrated by one of the characters or by an all-seeing ('omniscient') narrator?
- Does the same person tell the story all the way through? Or do we see the events through the minds and feelings of a number of different people?
- Which characters does the narrator like? Which characters do you like or dislike? Do your sympathies change during the course of the book? Why? When?
- Any piece of writing (including your notes and essays) is the result of thousands of choices. No book had to be written in just one way: the author could have chosen other words, other phrases, other characters, other events. How could the author of your novel have written the story differently? If events were recounted by a minor character how would this change the novel?

Studying on your own requires self-discipline and a carefully thought-out work plan in order to be effective. Good luck.

*Early life*   Louise Lawrence was born in Leatherhead, Surrey, in 1943. At the age of 12 she moved to the Forest of Dean where she went to Lydney Grammar School. When she left school she became an assistant librarian, 'from which came my love and respect for books, and my thirst for written knowledge'.

She married and had the first of her three children in 1963. The experience turned her to writing. 'Deprived of book-filled surroundings, I was bound to write my own.' As this time coincided with the real threat of nuclear war, it is likely that Louise Lawrence was affected by fears for her own children in an uncertain future. This may have laid the foundations for *Children of the Dust*, published several years later in 1985.

Since her O levels she has not received a formal education, but has taught herself. Among her interests are botany, poetry, religion, yoga, politics and the occult. 'Attempting to understand people led me to study psychology for many years – which led me to study feminism – which led to sociology. The road is endless.'

*Storytelling*   Louise Lawrence fondly remembers the time spent with her grandfather in the Forest of Dean and the stories he told her. When she was raising her children, she wrote stories to compensate for the loss of intellectual stimulation, and wrote as a 'way of escaping from an unhappy reality'. Although she claims that her early books were not good and she ended up burning them, they were the 'learning devices' that helped her write books that were published later. She wrote *Andra* from a 'film screen in my head' and a year later *The Power of Stars*, which was also published in America. *Children of the Dust* is 'a kind of culmination as far as my visionary capacities were concerned' and is certainly her most successful book to date.

The book came from a vision – 'I saw the nuclear war happening all around me and watched the characters play out their story'. Although she says that she did not wish to write about this subject, her children's activities in the Campaign for Nuclear Disarmament (a pressure group against nuclear warfare) and the real fear of nuclear war that existed then persuaded her to put pen to paper.

She never 'saw' another book in a vision again but has since written *Moonwind* and *The Warriors of Taan*. Although writing became more onerous to her, she wrote *Extinction is Forever* and *Ben-Harran's Castle*. After obtaining a computer, she produced *The Disinherited* and *Calling B for Butterfly*.

Louise Lawrence is still writing and still asking questions. Her vision of a pleasanter, kinder world is still explored in her books and 'Each book I write is a gift to whoever reads it. I hope they take from it what they will, if only a few hours of enjoyment'.

## CONTEXT & SETTING

*The threat of nuclear war*

The novel belongs to the 'post-apocalyptic' genre. This means that it is set in an imaginary era following a threat to human existence. Although there are examples of this type of literature before the twentieth century, it became a popular genre since the 1950s when the real threat of nuclear war became a major concern. To understand fully the context in which these books were written, it is important to understand the social and historical background of the time.

The Second World War saw considerable developments in military technology, the most destructive being the atom bomb. This was used against Japan by American

forces, but the scale of the destruction appalled many
people, especially when the photographs of Hiroshima
and Nagasaki became available and the true extent of
the horror created by these weapons was understood.

Although the Second World War came to an end in
Europe in May 1945 and in the Far East in August of
the same year, the development of nuclear weapons
continued and the feeling of distrust between the East
and the West grew. The 1950s, which saw the division
of Europe by the 'Iron Curtain' and the growing
antagonism between the capitalist West and the
Communist East, are generally known as the Cold War
years. Although there was an apparent peace, there was
fierce competition between the military intelligence of
the East and the West which was reflected in the 'spy'
novel popularised by John Le Carré and Graham
Greene. There was also intense competition in scientific
research for military purposes, and by the end of the
1960s many countries possessed the ability to use
nuclear weapons and the possible threat of mutual
destruction crept closer.

*Nuclear* Many people formed pressure groups such as CND
*disarmament* (Campaign for Nuclear Disarmament) and attracted
*protest groups* considerable media coverage for their various protests
against the development of nuclear arms. By making
speeches, writing articles and pamphlets, such groups
made the Western population intensely aware of the
possible danger of nuclear war. A controversial film was
privately circulated which simulated the effects of
nuclear war on a civilian population. It frightened
people who began to challenge the reasons for
developing such weapons.

Writers, artists and actors continued to express their
fears. It is a common practice amongst writers to use
fiction to criticise contemporary society, and a number

of books, plays, poems and films focused on what would happen if the world embarked on a nuclear war. As protest groups outlined the possible consequences of nuclear war and argued that few people would survive, it became important for governments on both sides to claim that whilst there would be casualties, the majority of people would survive. All through the 1960s and 1970s, a propaganda battle was waged between those who were against the development and possible use of nuclear weapons and those who were convinced that such weapons would maintain peace in an increasingly hostile confrontation between the East and the West.

The British government circulated a pamphlet outlining what to do in the event of a nuclear war. The nuclear disarmament pressure groups claimed that this advice was useless and only issued to pacify the population rather than help them. In Part 1 of *Children of the Dust*, we see Veronica putting this advice into practice, and while Catherine and Johnson survive, the majority of the characters do not. The pressure groups argued that people in power might have access to bunkers but the majority of the population would not reach safety, and of course this is described in Part 2 of the novel, 'Ophelia'.

During this time Raymond Briggs produced his famous book in strip cartoon form, *When the Wind Blows* (H. Hamilton, 1982; paperback, Penguin, 1983), an ironic comment on the futility of following the government guidelines. The two main cartoon characters are an ageing couple, stereotypes of ordinary people, who believe what they are told by the authorities and act upon this advice. As we watch them fall sick and finally die, we are forced to realise how their simple trust has been misplaced. (The book or the film version of it would be useful to look at as it illustrates what happens in the first part of *Children of the Dust*.)

*Change of*
*political*
*climate*

By the mid-1970s nuclear weapons became a major
political theme. Pressure groups grew in number and in
size of membership. The cost of developing and making
these weapons became difficult to maintain when the
world began to enter economic recession. Even those
who agreed with nuclear weapons became more
concerned as smaller and possibly less stable nations
gained the ability to use such arms and the threat to
world safety became a very real one. The political map
has changed since then, particularly in Eastern Europe,
and the end of the Cold War has diminished the threat
of nuclear war. Fewer books have used the background
of nuclear war but *Children of the Dust* is still relevant in
its discussion of tolerance, difference and evolution.

# TIMELINE

### 1 THE SECOND WORLD WAR

- The invention, development and testing of the nuclear bomb in Hiroshima and Nagasaki
- The final division of Europe into East and West
- The political and economic conflict between Western capitalism and Eastern Communism
- The intensification of the Cold War

### 2 THE 1950S AND 1960S

- The universal fear of nuclear war
- The growing protest movement against nuclear weapons
- The use of literature and the arts to inform people about the dangers of nuclear weapons

### 3 THE 1970S AND 1980S

- Economic recession throughout the world
- The economic impossibility of maintaining an arms race and the decline of Communism in Eastern Europe
- Increasing civilian concern over nuclear weapons
- Cracks in the solidity of the European Communist block and the growth of capitalism

### 4 THE 1990S

- The final collapse of European Communism
- The growth of regionalism, ethnic divisions and conflicts
- The invention of 'ethnic cleansing'
- The paradoxical attempt to create a unified Europe
- Concern with racism, prejudice and ignorance

# PART TWO

# SUMMARIES

## GENERAL SUMMARY

The book is in three parts, each covering a particular time and concentrating on a set of particular **characters** (see Literary Terms). The link between the parts is the relationship of some of the characters.

***Part 1: Sarah (pp. 1–60)*** Part 1 begins with the outbreak of nuclear war. Sarah is sent home from school. Her stepmother Veronica's main aim now is to protect her two children, Catherine and William, as far as possible. She prepares the house against the blast as instructed by the government and stocks up on food and water. The family dog is left outside. The precautions taken by Veronica are not sufficient: she herself, Sarah and William fall ill, victims of radioactive fall-out. Veronica and Sarah concentrate on the survival of the younger daughter, Catherine, who is not affected.

Veronica leaves the house and goes to the church to die. Sarah, knowing that she too is ill, takes Catherine to Johnson, who is also a 'survivor'. He promises to look after Catherine.

***Part 2: Ophelia (pp. 61–114)*** Part 2 again starts with the outbreak of nuclear war. Catherine's father, Bill Harnden, gives a lift to a woman, Erica Kowlanski, a scientist who takes him to the safety of a nuclear bunker, a protective nuclear shelter. Most of the people there are politicians, scientists, Army and Air Force chiefs, administrators. If the bunker society is to survive, women of child-bearing age must produce children. Bill assumes that all his family is dead and marries Erica who gives birth to a daughter, Ophelia.

The bunker is under the general control of General MacAllister who has a vision of re-creating twentieth-century society as it was. Bill Harnden is not totally happy with the politics of the bunker society and tries to instil some understanding of the importance of art and basic skills. However, MacAllister will not accept any opposition and punishes those who challenge his authority. Colonel Allison's son Dwight is taught by Bill and agrees with his ideas. Unlike his teacher, he believes in rebellion and after painting an anti-MacAllister slogan, he is sent away to work clearing out the septic tanks.

MacAllister decides that the community needs to 'requisition' animals from the survivors outside the bunker. Bill and Dwight do not agree that it is moral to take the outside survivors' resources and leave the bunker to warn them.

Ophelia joins Bill and Dwight on their journey to warn the outsiders and finds herself meeting her stepsister, Catherine, who has survived the war, married Johnson and is now horribly deformed through her exposure to radiation. She gives birth to a child called Allison (after Colonel Allison) who is a mutant. Ophelia returns to the bunker with her father, leaving Dwight outside.

*Part 3: Simon (pp. 115–68)*    In Part 3, Ophelia's son, Simon, is taking part in an expedition from the bunker to trade with the outside people (now mutated and called 'the mutants'). He meets by accident a mutated girl called Laura and, following an accident to his leg, is taken to her settlement. There he realises that Laura is his cousin. This part of the novel is concerned with Simon's feelings about his own people from the bunker and the mutants. When he realises that he is less able to survive than they are he remembers his mother's judgement that the bunker people are 'dinosaurs'. Angry and humiliated, he leaves the mutants' village.

*(pp. 1–19)*

He is attacked by savage dogs and escapes to barricade himself into a church. He is spotted by a glider plane from the mutants' village, and rescued by Laura. He is taken by her to see the Abbey Dwight Allison had built. He understands at last that the world and the outsiders have evolved into something more special than his own people could be. He has learned about differences, about sharing and about a new way of living. He also realises that, despite the fact that he cannot live unaided outside the bunker, he can contribute to the new world just as Dwight had done in building the beautiful Abbey. The book ends with Simon acknowledging his own worth and his intention to contribute to the future.

## DETAILED SUMMARIES

PART 1 SARAH

*Pages 1–19*
*The explosion*

The book opens with the description of a perfect day offering a picture of tranquillity and peace. The reality is exactly the opposite. We are given a brief account of the chaos and fear created by the news of an imminent nuclear attack but the main focus is on the fifteen-year-old Sarah's thoughts and feelings. We are quickly introduced to Sarah's stepmother Veronica and her stepsister Catherine and stepbrother William. Sarah's father, Bill Harnden, is away teaching at Bristol University. Veronica is frantically trying to follow the government guidelines to help her family survive, while William and Catherine who are too young to understand are treating the situation like a game.

Veronica puts Buster, the dog, outside and the family barricade themselves in and wait for the explosion. The broadcast instructions to 'Stay in your houses' (p. 10) until the radiation levels die down soon become futile when basic issues like toilet facilities and water are considered. It is obvious that at government level not enough time or thought had been given to the preparations. The nuclear explosion is described as Sarah experienced it, its horror contrasting with the howling of the dog outside. After the explosion, the relationship between Veronica and her stepdaughter

Sarah is discussed, and we gain more knowledge about the personalities of William and Catherine. Veronica and Sarah question whether it is better to live or to die under these circumstances, and they conclude that their purpose must be to ensure that the two younger children survive.

COMMENT

*Look at the way the writer describes the explosion as a living being attacking the natural environment.*

The book uses a device called **pathetic fallacy** (see Literary Terms) in reverse. Instead of mirroring human tragedy, nature remains indifferent to it to the end. A world disaster is happening at the height of summer. It is a beautiful day, and yet the world as people know it will end.

The conflict which exists in the Harnden family is a small version of the conflict which caused the war between nations. In Part 3, by contrast, we shall find kindness and generosity in the community of mutants, in their personal relationships, and in their attitude to other communities.

*(pp. 19–26)*

GLOSSARY

**Hamburg and Leningrad** the fate of two major cities in Western and Eastern Europe indicates the scale of the war

**sanitary** in this case toilet and cleaning arrangements

**sanctuary** a place of safety

**And this is the way the world ends ... a whimper** Veronica is quoting from T.S. Eliot's (1888–1965) poem 'The Hollow Men'

*Pages 19–26*
*The day after*

*Sarah's growing*
*understanding of*
*Veronica.*

Buster has been left outside to die of radiation poisoning and William does not understand why the dog cannot come inside. In these pages we are shown the conflict arising out of living together in such conditions as tension begins to build up. Sarah is faced with the fact that if Veronica cannot cope she will have to take her place. In a reversal of their roles Sarah takes command, enlisting the younger children's help to tidy up the room while Veronica questions the value of trying to keep up 'civilised standards' (p. 25). Catherine insists that she intends to survive, sheltered by her 'house' under the table.

COMMENT

The story is told mainly through Sarah, as we share her thoughts and reactions. Her understanding of her possible future role comes as Veronica appears less and less able to make decisions or be firm with William, particularly over Buster (feeding the dog will begin Veronica's illness). The reduction of Veronica's role in the narration and Sarah's dominance indicate what will happen to Veronica before the end of this part.

It is interesting to look at the way in which the author compares the possible future with descriptions of the environment.

*Pages 26–38*
*Another day*

The time has become less specific; it could be the following morning, but equally several days may have passed. This day begins by focusing on the shared purpose of preparing Veronica to go outside.

| | |
|---|---|
| *Catherine and William* | There are more references to Catherine's possible survival rather than to William's, indicating that he might not survive. Veronica provides an account of 'outside' and of the effect of the radioactive fallout. The reader grows aware that Veronica will not survive as she 'dully' (p. 31) insists on being the one to feed Buster despite Sarah's grim offer. Her movements are |
| *How is Catherine made 'special'?* | described as apathetic (p. 31), and it becomes obvious that she is already beginning to suffer the effects of radiation poisoning. Her purpose is weakening with the advance of her sickness, and it becomes clear that survival will depend on Sarah. It is interesting though that William's safety appears less important. Veronica's final collapse throws the weight of responsibility on to Sarah. |
| *Radiation sickness* | They realise that the room is contaminated (p. 35), and only Catherine remains a possible survivor. After the first shock of the discovery, Veronica and Sarah seem to share a new sense of purpose, with Veronica producing a pack of cards for the children and cooking a proper meal. With the two younger children asleep, Veronica and Sarah discuss Catherine's instinctive determination to survive. |
| COMMENT | The focus on Catherine's survival instinct and William's impetuous nature allows the reader to predict what is going to happen. Veronica's bin-liner protective suit is almost a parody of protective clothing. We might remember it when we come to Part 2 where those in authority who had played a part in bringing about the war are shown to have more effective protection than the rest of the population. |
| *God* | Through Sarah, we are reminded of the importance of belief in God and a sense of higher purpose and possible redemption from the situation created by people. This is important in the novel, particularly in Part 3. Conflict between Sarah and Veronica has |

virtually disappeared in their shared purpose – to save
Catherine at least

GLOSSARY
**radioactive fallout** as atomic bombs explode, they give out
radiation which enters the atmosphere. Radioactive dust
settles on the ground and permeates the air as 'fall-out'. It is
highly radioactive and therefore life-threatening
**Strip-Jack-naked** a simple card game popular with children

*Pages 38–53*  Sarah and Veronica plan an expedition to replenish
*Days pass*    their supplies. Veronica finally returns with Farmer
               Arkwright who has survived the initial blast. He shoots
*Buster dies*  the dying Buster.

Veronica describes the situation outside; everything has
been looted. But the donation of some supplies from
other survivors at the church, and eggs and milk from
the farm suggest that there is still some compassion and
kindness left in the remains of society. This, of course,
is vital in understanding Part 2, where we see the
growth of a peaceful community outside the bunker.
Veronica also brings packets of seeds for Catherine's
future.

She herself and Sarah both accept that they will die,
and eat contaminated food to make sure that Catherine
can have the remaining tinned supplies. Sarah accepts
her responsibility. It becomes obvious that they will kill
themselves by taking an overdose rather than suffer.

The remainder of this section describes the deaths
outside the house, which include the suicide of Farmer
Arkwright and his wife, and Veronica's suffering from
radiation poisoning. Sarah attempts to find
uncontaminated supplies to add to the seeds for
Catherine's future. At the farm she finds healthy calves
and barricades them in to save them for Catherine. She
takes a gun from Farmer Arkwright's dead hands, and
acknowledges that in time she will suffer as Veronica is

suffering. William too is beginning to display the symptoms of poisoning.

*Veronica dies*     Veronica leaves to go to church and dies there.

COMMENT     The necessity to believe in something turns Sarah to the Bible, and the blame for what has happened is firmly laid on the people in power. The bleak descriptions of the outside and of the reactions of the dwindling population mirror the biblical stories of purging the world of sin. The story is still being told from Sarah's viewpoint and contains references to God and spiritual matters. God becomes important now as the family discuss responsibility and accountability. Sarah is reading the story of Noah, and the biblical parallel of purging the world of evil becomes obvious particularly when Catherine announces that all the serpents have died in the nuclear war. Clearly the possibility of the nuclear war being a modern 'flood' is indicated.

*Pages 53–60*     This section forms the conclusion to Part 1. Veronica is
*A few weeks*     gone, William's condition continues to deteriorate and
*pass*     Sarah too is showing clear symptoms of radiation sickness. Finally, she realises that she must take Catherine to a safe place and, leaving William by himself, they leave the house. The description of people they meet is almost surreal. They recognise neighbours who seem to have lost their humanity. They are dying and desperate and have been reduced to selfish thieves.
*Meeting*     Yet a neighbour, Mrs Porter, acknowledges that Sarah
*survivors*     and Catherine should be left alone and persuades her husband to allow them to leave. Thus unknowingly she plays a part in Catherine's survival as does her husband who mentions Johnson to them.

*Johnson takes*     Although Catherine does not want to go, Sarah is
*Catherine*     aware that Johnson remains her only hope for Catherine's survival. The dying Sarah leaves Catherine

*(pp. 53–60)*

**Sarah and**
**William die**
with him and returns home to William where they will take pills to die easily.

COMMENT
There is a sense of finality about the tone and style of the writing here. Information is given from Sarah's perspective only, and we see the last of Catherine as a little girl. Catherine's survival dominates this section. William is left alone so that Sarah can ensure Catherine's safety and even Mrs Porter and her husband Ted unwittingly contribute to her survival, their actions emphasising Johnson's belief that there is a higher authority with a will.

GLOSSARY
**lich gate**  roofed churchyard gate for resting the coffin on the way to a funeral

**a brave new world**  a quotation from William Shakespeare's *The Tempest*, Act V, Scene 1. It is also the ironical title of a novel by Aldous Huxley (1894–1963) which describes a world not unlike MacAllister's bunker

# TEST YOURSELF (Part 1)

## A ··· *Identify the speaker.*

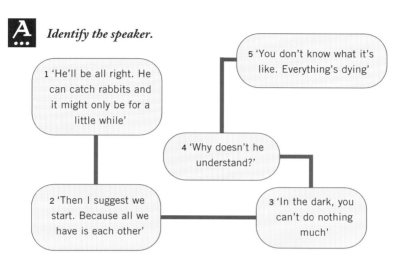

5 'You don't know what it's like. Everything's dying'

1 'He'll be all right. He can catch rabbits and it might only be for a little while'

4 'Why doesn't he understand?'

2 'Then I suggest we start. Because all we have is each other'

3 'In the dark, you can't do nothing much'

## *Identify 'to what or whom' this comment refers.*

6 'I expect he's dead'

7 'I'll look after her, I'll teach her to grow'

Check your answers on page 69.

## B ··· *Consider these issues.*

**a** Lawrence contrasts man-made destruction with the natural world. Look at how this view influences her opinion of events.

**b** Look at the tensions that exist in the family, and how when faced with destruction, the family are united in the attempt to make sure that Catherine survives.

**c** God is introduced, bringing comfort to the dying. Look at all the references that suggest that the war is a form of purging.

**d** Examine the different ways survivors behave, particularly Johnson, the people from the church and Mr and Mrs Porter.

PART 2    OPHELIA

*Pages 63–9*    This section begins at the same time as Part 1 – on the
*Day of*    day of the explosion – and Bill Harnden, who is the
*nuclear*    father of Sarah from Part 1, is introduced. His car is
*explosion*    flagged down by Erica Kowlanski, a scientist who
promises him a place in a nuclear bunker in exchange
for a lift.

*The survivors*    The survivors who are described as high-ranking Army
*in the bunker*    and Air Force personnel (both British and American),
civic dignitaries, civil servants, scientists, contrast with
Catherine and Johnson. The contrast foreshadows the
future conflict in Part 3. These people maintain the
power structures and organisation systems that predate
the war. The fact that only two thirds of those who had
been allocated places, managed to reach the bunker
reminds the reader that even if survival was planned, it
was not always achieved.

Several years are covered in these pages, with
information given concerning the nuclear winter, the
flattened cities and the subzero temperatures which
prevent aerial surveys of the world outside the bunker.
We are told that people survived but that there was
sickness, mutation and cancer-related diseases which
would reduce the fragmented population even further.
General MacAllister, the man in charge of the bunker,
plans to restore Britain to what it had been before the
war.

The scientific process of survival is described and
Erica's role as an authority in cellular cloning becomes
important in the bunker people's attempts to grow food
and rear animals, all of whom are mutated in some
form. The priorities given to upholding authority now
seem misguided as people realise that they need to
produce children.

*Ophelia born*   Although there is no love or affection between them, Erica who is still just young enough, chooses Bill to be the father of her child probably because, unlike herself, he has the ability to love and rear children. Ophelia is born. She reminds Bill of Sarah. Other children are born, among them Wayne, brother to Dwight, children of the American Colonel Allison and his wife.

COMMENT   In this section, we are told the story from Bill's perspective to begin with, and immediately the question of whether he was lucky to be in the bunker is raised. Unlike the first part where a very detailed account of survival attempts is given, here we find a rapid summary of the weeks of army-like routine, and an account of Bill's low position.

The way in which the bunker survivors cling to their old methods of control and power, despite the lack of any need to do so, is described, and the rather pathetic flying Union Jack at the top of the bunker is shown to be an empty symbol of triumph. The writing reflects the feeling of isolation and lack of purpose that Bill feels. These first few pages act as a background to the life of Ophelia who will be a central **character** (see Literary Terms) in Part 2. Bill's choice of her name is significant as is the quotation from *Hamlet*, Act II, Scene 2, which acts as a reminder of the plight of the bunker people, and a warning for her future.

Once more the section compares the destruction of the world with nature, reminding the reader that on this same day Sarah rushed home from school through the beautiful Gloucestershire countryside. Just as in Part 1 the natural world is compared to the desolation created by human destruction, so the bunker offers an artificial and sterile comparison to nature.

Early in this section, we are introduced to the organisation and power structures of the bunker which

*(pp. 69–78)*

had already resulted in nuclear war and which contrast with the vision of a better world offered by Johnson in Part 1. The inability to develop successful clones from the 'legalised theft' (p. 68) of crops and animals from the survivors outside indicates that the bunker community cannot continue forever. There is implied criticism of government priorities which have excluded women and other powerless people.

GLOSSARY      **And let her not walk i' the sun** a quotation from William Shakespeare's *Hamlet*, Act II, Scene 2. Hamlet's words referring to Ophelia acquire a new meaning here; like the rest of the bunker people, Ophelia Harnden must not walk in the sun without protective clothing (see p. 67)

*Pages 69–78*   This section describes Ophelia's childhood, and the
*Some twenty*   bunker as seen through her eyes. She knows nothing
*years later*   except a military, technological world. The authorities are not interested in Bill's teaching of literature and history of the world. Ophelia's friend Dwight Allison begins to challenge the views and authority of his
*Conflicts in*  father, Colonel Allison, and General MacAllister. The
*the bunker*    outside seen from the telescreens is described as infertile, with no survivors nearby, and the attempts to start farming a little further away from the bunker produce only mutants. The bunker is taking what it wants from the survivors outside using government requisition orders. This ruthless requisitioning will become important later on in this part of the novel.

COMMENT      Although life goes on in the bunker, there is evidence that it will not always do so despite Ophelia's confidence. The cracks in the concrete and the crumbling structure suggest the eventual collapse of life in the bunker.

There is a growing conflict about priorities between those represented by Bill and Dwight Allison and those in authority. Bill and Dwight believe in creating things, in imagination and in art. The authorities believe that workers will be recruited from the outside and that science and technology should dominate. The growing differences of opinion distance Dwight from Ophelia who does not really accept his brother Wayne's assertion that Dwight's rebelliousness is part of growing up, and blames her father's teaching.

Constant references to survivors suggest that outsiders must have been successful to some extent at least in producing their own crops and livestock, despite their lack of protective clothing and shelter and absence of technology, which makes the bunker's failure all the more significant.

GLOSSARY

**sceptred isles … seas** quotation from William Shakespeare's *Richard II*, Act II, Scene 1

**seasons of mist and … fruitfulness** a quotation from John Keats's (1745–1821) poem 'To Autumn'

**He could design the city of the future** a pointer to Dwight's design for the beautiful Abbey described in Part 3 (p. 159)

*Pages 79–90*
*Some days*
*later*

*Dwight's*
*rebellion*

Ophelia is not part of the growing resistance and is not present when Dwight writes his insulting message to General MacAllister on the wall. At sixteen she is separated from him when he is sentenced to twelve months' labour cleaning the septic tanks. Ophelia finds herself in the middle of the argument between her father who recognises the danger signals of the MacAllister regime and her mother who accepts the rule. Unusually it is her mother who understands Ophelia's loss when Dwight is banished but she argues too that women do not necessarily need men to be happy. Dwight's departure has also split the young dissenters who drift aimlessly. Ophelia learns from her father of the existence of Veronica and Sarah, and the readers are reminded of them as well.

*(pp. 79–90)*

**MacAllister plans to raid the outside**

When MacAllister learns of more communities and agricultural settlements outside, he decides that it is time to 'start looking outward' (p. 83). By this he apparently means taking the outsiders' livestock and placing it 'under government protection' (p. 83) which will help the continued survival of the bunker people. Dwight argues that this would reduce the chances of those living outside and that it is theft and cattle-rustling. The argument between Dwight and Erica about how resources are shared is a political debate on how to organise communities, and the reader is invited to agree with Dwight.

A turning point is reached when Dwight and Bill decide to take a truck and go to warn the outsiders of the oncoming raid by the bunker army. Ophelia, caught up in her need for both men, decides to join them. Dwight's father, although agreeing with his son, is an army officer and will carry out MacAllister's orders even if he disagrees with them. Dwight explains to Ophelia that they will not be able to return to the bunker after this action.

COMMENT

General MacAllister's speech to Bill's students is like something out of George Orwell's (1903–50) *Animal Farm* and is almost a parody of the ranting of a dictator. Ophelia and her father discuss respect and love, and Bill comments that 'However bad the experience we can always learn something from it' (p. 82), which is one of the main points of the novel.

Ophelia seems to be less positive as a **character** (see Literary Terms) than Sarah. Her acceptance of authority in the bunker is typical of those who choose not to think about the morality of decisions made by their leaders. That they might be wrong is established through Dwight and Bill directly.

Whilst the bunker is described as crumbling and running out of resources, the outside world, where people have had to survive using their own resources, is beginning to grow again. At this point we are reminded of Sarah's forward-looking observation at the end of Part 1 when she touches the gorse flower, and sees in it a symbol of hope.

*Pages 90–7*
*The next two*
*days*

This section concerns the trip to Johnson's settlement. We are given a description of Ophelia's discomfort due to travel sickness during the trip and Dwight's disregard for her feelings as he concentrates on his mission. Dwight's sense of purpose is almost manic.

*How are we*
*shown the world*
*outside?*

The outside landscape is now described as 'alien' (p. 90) but nature has returned. Ophelia is overwhelmed by sensory impressions as she sees insects, smells flowers and breathes air for the first time. Dwight brutally makes her realise the difficulty of living outside which will stress the bravery and persistence of the outsiders when we eventually meet them. When at last they do find the community they were looking for, Bill is amazed to recognise Johnson's place.

*Link with Part 1*
*established.*

The connection between Part 1 and Part 2 is now established and the reader is privileged above the characters in the novel who have yet to realise that

*(pp. 97–114)*

connection. The sight of the hideously scarred, disfigured, heavily pregnant woman who meets them, aiming her gun at Bill, prompts Ophelia to take off her visor and leave the truck. When the woman sees Ophelia's face, she greets her joyfully as her sister Sarah, and her own identity becomes obvious.

COMMENT    This section is told completely from Ophelia's viewpoint which is why we are given accounts of her feelings, discomfort and fear and only see the edge of Dwight's zealous mission. We also see, through her eyes, impressions of a landscape that she was never able to imagine. Once Bill recognises Johnson's place, the reader is in the privileged position of knowing that Bill will be reunited with his daughter Catherine.

The description of the outside shows rebirth. The promise Sarah sensed at the end of Part 1 is beginning to be fulfilled. That the outside world seems alien to Ophelia shows the lack of communication between the bunker people and the world outside. The differences between the outsiders' lives and those of the bunker people are made clear, and the readers are invited to take the part of the outsiders. Survival has taken place and what was predicted in Part 1 has been realised in Part 2.

GLOSSARY    **Telford's bridge** Thomas Telford (1757–1834), a brilliant architect who designed several remarkable bridges, mostly in the West of England

*Pages 97–114*    In this section we see a 'David and Goliath' fight
*The next day*    between the unarmed Johnson and Colonel Allison, brought to an end by Dwight's direct action of burning the trucks. We are given background details of how the outsiders survived in the years after the explosion and learned old trades within the idyllic community. The dream of communal living may now become reality.

*The future lies with the mutants.*

The dying Johnson is clearly loved but Ophelia can see only ugliness in the form of the symptoms of radiation exposure suffered by Catherine and Johnson. She is horrified by the sexual relationship between Catherine and Johnson, resulting in mutant children. Her perception of the 'garden' changes. The community of seven hundred people live in virtual squalor because, as Catherine reminds the visitors, the land must come before people. Dwight accepts the community's ideas readily and reminds Ophelia that their own civilisation is prepared to steal cattle. He argues, 'We're dinosaurs in a bunker! We deserve to become extinct!' (p. 101), a major theme of Part 3.

*Mutation necessary for survival.*

*Does the scientific explanation make the mutants acceptable?*

Catherine's description of genetic damage caused by radiation explains the six dead children she has borne. Lilith, her surviving daughter, a mutant, is introduced. She seems to see in a different way with her strangely blind-looking eyes, her body is covered with pale fur, her hair is white. Catherine gives birth to another mutant child. Dwight explains that only these children will survive – that they mutated genetically as a form of natural adaptation to the new environment.

The dairy cows cannot be moved to safety because they cannot be marched for long distances. This means that the attempt to stop Colonel Allison's men from taking the cows has failed. Dwight argues with his father about the morality of taking the cows. Johnson explains that they give other communities enough pregnant cows and a bull to start their own herds, and he is willing to do the same for the bunker people, but Allison's orders are to take all the cattle and he will not negotiate despite Bill's assertion that the bunker has no facilities for milking cows.

*Dwight saves the cattle*

Dwight sets the army trucks on fire and then disappears. Ophelia realises that he had always intended to stay – he believed that the future was with the outsiders. She knows, however, that she must return. Part 2 concludes with Lilith holding the baby, the future of the human race, in her arms, and smiling pityingly at Ophelia.

COMMENT

*Ophelia's view of the settlement.*

We are given the story from Ophelia's point of view and although she sees the ugliness in the community she can also see how good Johnson's ideas are. Although Ophelia is appalled and disgusted by the mutants, the description of Lilith is not unsympathetic, and we do not always share Ophelia's views. At the end of the section, Lilith with the new-born baby in her arms seems to point to the future and pity Ophelia.

The beauty of the outside world and Ophelia's views of it are still contrasted. Catherine's dream of the future is shown in the description of the valley growing green again, and the 'willowherb bloom[ing] sweet' (p. 101). Ophelia cannot understand the coexistence of hope and despair, beauty and ugliness, and we realise that Dwight, not she, will be part of this future.

*Conflict*

Conflict in this section occurs in two ways. Firstly the conflict of ideas and methods between Johnson and MacAllister is shown and we are encouraged to sympathise with Johnson. Although Johnson does not approve of violence, it is Dwight's violent action that prevents the cows being taken – another conflict of ideas. The conflict within Ophelia is described in full and we are made to understand that she will not share in the survival. The bunker people are 'dinosaurs' and their own existence is more under threat than that of the outsiders who have learned to adapt and come to terms with their new environment. Mutants like Lilith and the new baby are the result of the adaptation process. Ophelia's disgust is part of the old ways which will continue into Part 3 with the problems Simon has in coming to terms with Laura.

GLOSSARY     **Blake's Jerusalem** the poet William Blake's (1767–1827) vision of a new, better England in his poem *Milton*

**Pansies for thoughts** the mad Ophelia speaks of 'pansies, that's for thoughts' in William Shakespeare's *Hamlet*, Act IV, Scene 5

## A  Identify the speaker.

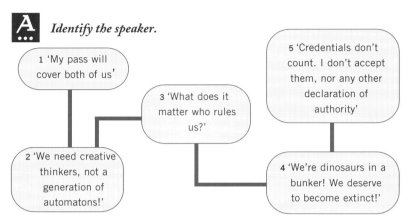

1 'My pass will cover both of us'

2 'We need creative thinkers, not a generation of automatons!'

3 'What does it matter who rules us?'

4 'We're dinosaurs in a bunker! We deserve to become extinct!'

5 'Credentials don't count. I don't accept them, nor any other declaration of authority'

## Identify the person 'to whom' this comment refers.

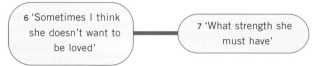

6 'Sometimes I think she doesn't want to be loved'

7 'What strength she must have'

Check your answers on page 69.

## B  Consider these issues.

**a** Look at the way the author is inviting us to criticise the rule of MacAllister in its attempt to reproduce the society that caused the war. Compare the different views expressed by Dwight, MacAllister, Erica and Bill.

**b** Throughout this section, there is a contrast between the old bunker society and the new, represented by the outside survivors. This is often reflected in descriptions of the environment. What is being said about progress here?

**c** Examine the way the author places MacAllister and Johnson in opposition to each other. Look at the role of Dwight as a rebel and Ophelia's position in the middle of the conflict. You may wish to think about the significance of her name.

**d** Look at the significance of the mutation that is occurring in the outside world. Think about the implications this has for the future and what this suggests about the nature of survival and evolution.

PART 3    SIMON

*Pages 117–34*    Simon, a member of the bunker community, is outside
*Fifty-five*    in the hills with two companions, Harris and Sowerby,
*years after the*    on an expedition to obtain supplies from the mutants
*nuclear*    outside the bunker. They see a person apparently being
*explosion*    attacked by dogs. They use guns to frighten them off
    but the person, Laura, prevents the dogs from hurting
*Simon meets*    her by using mind-control – a nonviolent means of
*Laura*    control. She is initially described by her external
    appearance which is strange. To begin with, Simon
    does not see her face and refers to her as 'the girl'.
    When he sees that she is mutated, he is horrified. Laura
    remains unnamed for several pages, an indication of
    Simon's view that she is not human.

    Simon gashes his leg on a rusty nail and has difficulty
    in walking over the rough ground, mainly because his
    worn shoes offer no protection. The reader realises now
    that the bunker people have lost basic skills such as
    shoe-mending. Throughout the section, Simon is
    shown as unable to accept the pity shown to him by the
    mutants. He has been brought up to believe that he is
    superior yet he is aware that people are dying in the
    bunker. The constant references to his mother hint that
    he is linked to the mutants in some way.

*The mutants*    Laura tells him that the mutants do not 'trade' – they
    give what others want, and Simon continually compares
    the situation of the bunker with the gentle civilisation
    of the mutants. Their ability to use their minds as a
    source of energy confuses him. He wonders whether
    they are superhuman, rather than subhuman. The
    mutants have created a new world – their calendar
    starting from the beginning of the war, fifty-five years
*Can you find*    ago – and they see themselves as chosen. Simon feels
*echoes of Johnson's*    humiliated by Laura's belief that her people are
*beliefs here?*    superior.

*(pp. 117–34)*

The first building Simon sees when he arrives at Laura's community is the communal living house (spoken of by Catherine in Part 2, p. 99) and the comparison he makes between the beautiful but functional place and his own crumbling environment hurts him and he loses consciousness. His medical treatment by the mutants is based on holistic, alternative medicine, and Lilith and Johnson are mentioned, reminding us of Parts 1 and 2.

*Simon meets blind Kate*

As Simon cannot walk, Harris and Sowerby intend to leave without him but his intolerance of the mutants, especially Lilith who frightens him, prevents him from accepting their help. Eventually Harris hits him and the two men leave without him. When he regains consciousness he sees an old woman who turns out to be Catherine, fifty-five years after Part 1. He does not know as yet that she is his aunt. Compared to Catherine, Laura now appears more acceptable physically.

'Blind Kate', as they now call Catherine, wants to know whether Simon knew Colonel Allison, and is obviously anxious for news of her half-sister Ophelia. Simon realises the connection (p. 134): blind Kate's half-sister, Ophelia, is his mother, and Laura's home is the place which his mother visited. Laura is his cousin but he cannot accept the relationship and he denies any knowledge of Ophelia.

COMMENT

These pages continually compare the bunker people with the mutants and contrast the two groups' philosophies. The bunker people had held on to twentieth-century standards but had no basic skills to help them survive once their raw materials disappeared. The war is now seen as an analogy to Noah's flood and the various biblical accounts of purges and of chosen survivors. The author concentrates on differences

between the two peoples and Simon's feelings about
them.

GLOSSARY

**Celtic** belonging to an old period in British history when
Stonehenge was supposed to have been built
**cromlech** stone circle
**monolith** massive stone pillar
**As it was in the beginning … ever shall be** a quotation from the
Book of Common Prayer
**lockjaw** another name for tetanus

*Pages 134–44*
*The next day*

Simon feels anger and pain at the differences he
experiences in the community. He feels guilty that the
bunker people had never cared what happened to the
outsiders, and yet it is the outsiders who are feeding
him and caring for him. The mutants' curiosity and pity
make him feel a freak, and he grows angrier still. He
rejects Laura because he is angry with his own people
and he realises that they cannot survive as the mutants
can. The more he learns, the more he realises that
everything that they had done in the bunker was useless
and he is angry because he feels that his future has been
sacrificed. He is angry because he is suffering for
something that he had not done.

*Simon's guilt*
*and*
*frustration*

*Discuss the causes*
*of Simon's anger.*

*Blind Kate*
*angry with*
*Simon*

When blind Kate comes to him, bringing food and
clothing, he sees what he will become and he hates her
because of that. She is also angry at his attitude, and
disgusted with his rejection of her granddaughter. Her
outburst pays him back for his cruelty to the
granddaughter she loves.

*Simon*
*attacked by*
*dogs*

Simon decides that he will leave, hoping to meet up
with his two companions. He encounters savage dogs
and realises that he cannot reach the sanctuary of a
distant church. A glider plane distracts the dogs,
enabling him to reach the church. He automatically
believes it must belong to the bunker people. After
barricading himself in, he realises that he is trapped and

that the wound in his leg is bleeding again. He has to accept that he has behaved stupidly but hopes that the glider plane can report his position to the bunker people who will come and rescue him.

COMMENT    Through this section we are given more knowledge of Laura's community and although it is seen through Simon's eyes, the reader is encouraged to consider it better than the pre-holocaust society and considerably kinder than the bunker society. Simon's aggressive attitude towards the mutant community shows us how those who are prejudiced are victims of their own feelings. The reader sees Simon as short-sighted and narrow but the emotional pain he suffers also creates sympathy for him. Although he accepts the clothing and the food, he rejects Laura's assistance and this causes her obvious pain. In the dining hall, he realises for the first time what it is like to be different. Although the mutants are pleasant, the parents have to explain to their children that Simon is not an animal and that people were all like him once, reinforcing the idea that it is Simon who is 'ape-like' rather than Laura who has evolved into something better. Through Simon, we learn that what hurts is his loss of the hope that the bunker people still have, that in time they will be able to survive.

GLOSSARY     **Homo sapiens**  man, human being (Latin for 'wise man')

**Neanderthal man**  primitive man of the Stone Age (named after Neanderthal in Germany where his bones were found)

*Pages 144–62*
*The day after*

*Laura saves*
*Simon*

*Simon comes to*
*terms with*
*himself.*

Simon wakes to hear Laura who has ridden a horse to find him. She sends the dogs away by mind control and somehow has the strength to move the barricade. She confronts him with his prejudice and when he looks at her, he realises that she is beautiful. Their discussion of the situation shows Simon's problem with his identity and his inability to accept his uselessness. She agrees to take him to Timperley on the horse and he is amazed at her strength as she lifts him up. They camp for the night at Devil's Pulpit because Laura wishes to show him the view which makes Simon angry. He learns that Laura and her people have telepathic communication and that the glider plane is powered by psycho-kinetic energy. He is changed by the view of the Abbey at Timperley and realises that he may have a part to play, just as Dwight Allison did, when he built it.

COMMENT     This section is one of trial and learning for Simon. During his walk he sees the countryside around him and convinces himself that Laura's settlement is just a simple rural community and that the mutants are not better than himself. His inability to cope with the change encourages him to think negatively and he begins his journey to find Harris and Sowerby.

After his rescue from the dogs Simon realises that it is himself who is his enemy – that the bunker people will need to accept that the outside survivors are the people of the future. This of course, is the message of the novel and Simon comes to understand that he is not responsible for what his ancestors had done.

GLOSSARY     **telepathy**  wordless communication between minds

*(pp. 163–end)*

*Pages 163–end*  Simon returns to Laura's settlement, a different person,
*Later the same*  more understanding and at peace with himself. He has
*day*       to wear protective clothing but he is freer now than
            ever. All his physical needs will be provided for and he
            has the freedom to contribute his own skills. His mind
*How does Simon*  races around the possibilities of using his technical
*see his future*  knowledge to develop aerial and space flight using
*now?*      psycho-kinetic energy but the real change occurs when
            he offers to share the horse with Laura and holds out
            his hand to her.

            He confesses that he lied to blind Kate and explains
            that his cruelty is due to his being human. He promises
            to apologise to Kate. It is his turn to ask for forgiveness
            and Laura accepts.

COMMENT     This is an important section in understanding the
            message of the book. Simon learns that he has a place
            in this community; he comes to terms with the faults of
            his predecessors and looks optimistically to having a
            role in the new future with the mutants.

GLOSSARY    **gestalt**  organised whole
            **Boyle's law**  the pressure exercised by a gas is in inverse ratio to
               its volume (formulated by Robert Boyle in the seventeenth
               century)
            **Einstein's theory of relativity**  all motion is relative, velocity of
               light is always constant relative to an observer. The theory was
               formulated by Albert Einstein (1879–1955)

# TEST YOURSELF (Part 3)

## A Identify the speaker.

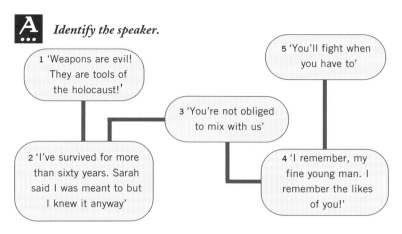

1 'Weapons are evil! They are tools of the holocaust!'

5 'You'll fight when you have to'

3 'You're not obliged to mix with us'

2 'I've survived for more than sixty years. Sarah said I was meant to but I knew it anyway'

4 'I remember, my fine young man. I remember the likes of you!'

### Identify the person 'to whom' this comment refers.

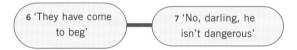

6 'They have come to beg'

7 'No, darling, he isn't dangerous'

Check your answers on page 69.

## B Consider these issues.

a This section discusses 'differences' between people. Think about the physical differences between Simon and Laura and the differences in the way in which they view the world. With whom do you sympathise and how far has the author influenced you?

b In this section Simon learns a lot about tolerance and evolution. Look carefully at what this means and what lessons could be learned from it.

c There is a continual contrast in this section between the physical power of weapons and destruction and the positive power of the mind and community. Look carefully at the way in which the author presents this.

d Most of the section is concerned with the relationship between Laura and Simon. Think about whether this could suggest a future relationship between different people and societies.

# COMMENTARY

## THEMES

### SURVIVAL

Although Louise Lawrence's 'vision' was depressing, her intention to produce a positive ending is evident through the novel.

*Survival of nature and people*

Survival appears unlikely following a nuclear war, but Johnson and Catherine survive and Part 1 emphasises Catherine's intention to survive which Sarah never doubts. There are constant references to nature surviving the calamity brought about by people, the gorse flower at the end of Part 1 being the dominant **image** (see Literary Terms). In Part 2 we witness the struggle of both the bunker people and those outside the bunker to survive the nuclear winter and Catherine tells us how difficult it was. In Part 3, it is the bunker people who are in danger of extinction, but Simon represents those who will survive – by becoming a part of the community outside; by accepting their help and giving what skills are required to progress.

*Survival of cultural heritage*

Underlying the survival of nature and people, is the idea of the survival of things from the past that are valuable. The Celtic cross survives the nuclear blast, as does Stonehenge. Ancient skills of weaving, building and medicine are preserved and developed by the survivors and paranormal activities which we tend to associate with the 'New Age' also develop. This creates a sense of optimism as a more idyllic society emerges from the dust.

You might also have noticed the use of quotations from the Bible and from English literature, especially Shakespeare, which indicate that this valuable part of the English heritage will also survive.

## FATE AND DESTINY

Throughout the novel, there is a suggestion that there is something bigger than human beings. In Part 1, Sarah frequently refers to God and nature. Her determination that Catherine will survive at all costs with its implicit acceptance of self-sacrifice (eating contaminated food, for instance, so that Catherine can have tinned food which is safe) may be regarded as a religious act. Veronica's departure to the church to die may also be seen as an acknowledgement of God's presence. The flowers that grow are positive signs that the world will continue, even if the environment and the people change. Sarah in Part 1 recognises that Catherine has a place in a divine scheme and that she must survive. Johnson, too, is aware of a design above human criminal folly (p. 59). Catherine in Part 2 speaks a lot about future society being organised on the basis of different values of collaboration and peace, which seems to come true in Part 3. Ideas of fate and destiny are closely linked to evolution, and the link between God and human survival through evolution is already established in Part 1, instinctively felt by Sarah and given expression to by Johnson.

*Does God play a part in the revival of hope?*

## EVOLUTION

Throughout the novel, there are many references to things evolving. The flower that ends Part 1, blooms for the future, 'radiate[s] the glory of God' (p. 60) and Sarah's belief that some things could not be destroyed becomes reality in the last part.

*Evolution by mutation*

The idea of evolving, of changing and developing is given through the contrast of the bunker people whom Dwight describes as 'dinosaurs in a bunker' (p. 101) with the survivors outside who are beginning to mutate. General MacAllister's intention to preserve twentieth-

century society is described unsympathetically by the
writer, and we are asked to agree with her that this
system is outdated, unhelpful and unjust. Dwight is
used to voice these opinions. In Part 2, the
confrontation between the bunker people and the
survivors is made more obvious when Colonel Allison
comes to take the cows and Johnson and Catherine
describe their way of living. In Part 3, the idea of
evolution is developed further. First, Simon is forced to
consider Laura as a developed human being rather than
the 'ape-girl' (p. 123) he initially describes. Secondly, he
realises that skills and organisations have evolved to
something superior to what he has grown used to, and,
finally, he discovers that he himself too has to evolve, to
develop and come to understand.

## PREJUDICE AND DIFFERENCE

Implicit in the novel is the idea of tolerance and insight
and, by contrast, of conflict and destruction. The war
begins because of conflict between different nations.
At the beginning of Part 2, we are reminded that
everyone has lost the war and that the pathetic flag
hoisted on the top of the bunker is meaningless. We
witness also Bill Harnden's struggles against the blind
prejudice of the bunker leaders in Part 2, and Ophelia's
intolerance of the differences to be seen in Catherine
and Lilith and her own inability to cope with these.
There are many references to sight, to seeing and of
course this can be seen as *insight*, knowledge and
understanding. Ophelia may never have finally
understood although she repeats to her son Simon
Dwight's words, 'dinosaurs in a bunker' (p. 121),
showing that she did have some insight. In Part 3, we

*Can you trace the* share Simon's struggle as he tries to come to terms with
*changes in Simon's* the differences after his initial prejudiced view of
*attitude to Laura?* Laura's appearance.

## SOCIAL ORGANISATION

In Part 1, eight-year-old Catherine speaks of remaking the Garden of Eden without the serpents which destroyed the original one (p. 45). Also in Part 1 Johnson tells Sarah that he and Catherine together will build a new world, a decent, free society, without violence, based on cooperation (p. 59).

In Part 2 we see this society in the process of being built. No longer based on the nuclear family system, it is rooted in cooperation, sharing, the communal spirit. As Catherine says to her father 'Right from the beginning, however little we had, we always shared it' (p. 99). And when we meet her again in Part 3, it appears that the society she and Johnson had dreamt of and worked for has become reality. This suggests that Catherine's 'tribe' was indeed 'chosen'.

*Two contrasting social organisations*
From Part 1, when we read of Catherine's intention to rid the world of serpents in the new Garden of Eden that she will create, the different ways of organising society are contrasted. General MacAllister organises the bunker in the same way that society was organised before the explosion. Dwight argues against this form of organisation, claiming it to be unfair and inefficient in the struggle for survival. He takes direct action against it and finally joins the survivors because of his beliefs. Catherine and Johnson argue a case for collaborative living. They give what they can without trading in exchange, in order to help everyone, including the bunker people, to survive, and this is the model for the future society that Simon meets in Part 3. Laura's community is a 'Utopian' one. It is an ideal society, built on peace, collaboration and equality. By existing, it criticises the traditional society preserved in the bunker.

# STRUCTURE

The book's three parts effectively tell the story of three different eras and generations. Parts 1 and 2 overlap as both start on the same day which enables us to explore the different experiences of members of the same family. There are very subtle references in all three parts that remind the reader of the connection between them. For example, in Part 1, 'Sarah', we are told of her father's photograph which looks down from the mantelpiece, and Part 2, 'Ophelia', then begins with the experiences of Sarah's father on the same day. When Ophelia meets Catherine, the other surviving member of the family from Part 1, the family connection through Ophelia's father is made. Simon's recognition of the connection in Part 3 also helps link Parts 2 and 3.

*Family links as part of the structure.*

It is important to remember the family connections. Sarah and Catherine from Part 1 are the daughters of Bill Harnden from Part 2, whose youngest daughter Ophelia leaves the bunker with her father and her friend Dwight Allison to warn the settlers whose leaders turn out to be Catherine and Johnson, the man into whose care she was entrusted by the dead Sarah. Simon from Part 3 is Ophelia's son. The family connection is very important when the theme of understanding and acceptance of difference is considered.

Another way of linking the parts is through events. Parts 1 and 2 both deal with the nuclear explosion and its effect on people. Part 1 documents the experiences in a makeshift shelter in the home. This would be the experience of the majority of the population who had no special status. In Part 2 Bill Harnden has a different experience and survives because of his accidental meeting with Erica Kowlanski, the scientist who has the right to shelter in a nuclear bunker. Parts 2 and 3 both deal with the aftermath of survival. In Part 2 we

*Parallel events linking the parts.*

are given details of the rules and regulations of a bunker run on military lines which was protected from the nuclear blast, and we are invited to compare this with the 'natural' survival of Catherine and Johnson. Part 2 concentrates on the morality of leadership and ways of living, whilst Part 3 goes further by considering the issues of prejudice, natural development and evolution. It is from this part that we gain any optimism.

*The passage of time*

The passage of time is carefully documented. The author makes several references to ages and dates to enable the reader to grasp how long events have taken. Parts 1 and 2 start on the same day. Part 1 ends a few weeks later whereas Part 2 continues for a further twenty years during which time, as the author reminds the reader, despite the destruction of humanity, nature has survived, adapted and is regrowing. Part 3 begins after a further thirty-five years during which time mutation of humans has occurred and enabled life to continue, despite the altered environment.

# CHARACTERS

*Main characters as links between parts*

With the exception of Bill Harnden, Catherine, Johnson and Lilith, most characters appear in one part of the novel only. Sarah, William and Veronica all die during or at the end of Part 1, Ophelia, Dwight, Wayne and the army people do not appear again after Part 2 although we are aware that Ophelia is probably still alive when we meet her son Simon in Part 3. The characters that do appear in more than one section are those who are linked with the future. Bill Harnden is the father of both Catherine and Ophelia and the grandfather of both Simon and Laura who meet in Part 3. It is his philosophy and attitudes that help Dwight to leave the bunker, join the survivors and build the Abbey. Catherine, later known as blind Kate, acts

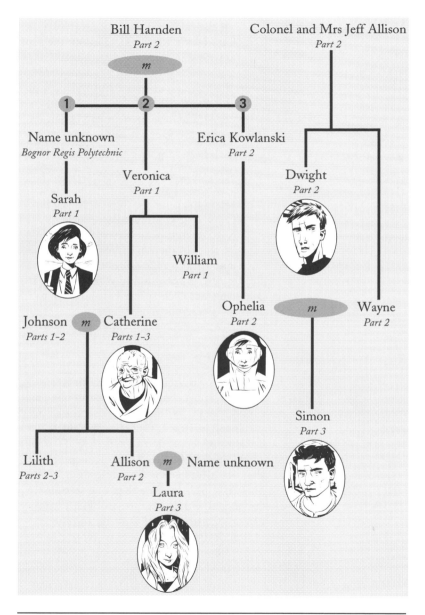

Bill Harnden
*Part 2*

Colonel and Mrs Jeff Allison
*Part 2*

m

**1**     **2**     **3**

Name unknown
*Bognor Regis Polytechnic*

Erica Kowlanski
*Part 2*

Dwight
*Part 2*

Veronica
*Part 1*

Sarah
*Part 1*

William
*Part 1*

Ophelia
*Part 2*

m

Wayne
*Part 2*

Johnson
*Parts 1–2*

m

Catherine
*Parts 1–3*

Simon
*Part 3*

Lilith
*Parts 2–3*

Allison
*Part 2*

m

Name unknown

Laura
*Part 3*

as a link between the past and the future, by giving birth to mutated babies, Lilith and Allison, whose daughter Laura, like Lilith, adapts to the new post-war environment. Laura, of course, represents the hope for a better future while Simon, representing the past, learns that he too must take part in the future. The family tree here will help understand the relationships.

To understand the leading characters, concentrate on how the writer presents them in the novel; imagine they are real people and form your own opinions of them. It is very important to make sure that you can show why you hold these views by referring closely to the text. Imagine that you know these characters. Do you like them? What do you admire about them? What do you dislike about them? Why?

You may wish to think about how you feel about the following characters.

## SARAH

*Responsible
Resourceful
and realistic*

Sarah is fifteen at the beginning of the book and is Bill's oldest daughter. She grows up very quickly in a few weeks and we see this through the changing relationship with Veronica, her stepmother. We are invited to consider what this relationship might have been like and how it has changed by the end of Part 1. Sarah becomes stronger as Veronica weakens. Much of Part 1 is told from Sarah's viewpoint and if we read it carefully, we shall gain more understanding of how she sees things. She is very observant and notices things.

In the Bible, Sarah, the wife of Abraham, demonstrates the power of faith when she helps found the tribe of Israel. Although Sarah in the novel dies, her faith in the future helps her keep Catherine alive. Because Part 1 is told from Sarah's viewpoint, we can see her as a dominant personality.

## CATHERINE

*Determined to survive*
*Strong and fiercely loyal*
*Cruelly truthful in Part 3*

Catherine is eight when the war starts in Part 1 and she links the three parts of the book. Although other characters are mentioned in more than one part, for instance Bill in Part 1, and again, with Dwight and Ophelia, in Part 3, Catherine is the only one who physically appears in each section of the book, linking the three stories.

*Why is Catherine special?*

She is, then, a key character. Read Part 1 very carefully and notice how determined she is to survive. For an eight-year-old, she says some very significant things about the future society she wishes to make (p. 44).

*Do you think that she has been chosen in some way?*

When she appears in Part 2, at 28, she shows signs of suffering from radiation exposure and is heavily pregnant with Johnson's child. She has already given birth to a mutant, Lilith, and her second child, Allison, is born while her father Bill, her half-sister Ophelia and Dwight Allison are visiting the settlement. Her role in this section seems to be to give birth to the new people who will mutate to adapt to the new environment produced by the war. She is the one who tells Bill and Dwight how the outsiders survived and how their society now works (pp. 98–9).

*What is Catherine's purpose in Part 2?*

She acts as a source of information in this section. Bill, Dwight, Ophelia and the reader learn from her about what has happened outside the bunker after the war. Look at how Catherine has grown and what kind of adult she has become. You may find it particularly helpful to reread what she has to say about creating a new society based on different values from the one that destroyed the world. Ophelia finds Catherine's 'great swollen stomach ... suddenly obscene' (p. 100). Reread page 102 and look at how the relationship between Johnson and Catherine is described by the author and how her description compares with Ophelia's initial view. The difference tells us more about Ophelia.

*Do you sympathise with Ophelia's view of Catherine?*

In Part 3, Catherine, now known as blind Kate, is an old woman. In fact she is only 63 but Simon's description of her on pages 131–2 is of a much older woman, a rotting hag. Although he is aware that she has lived through the nuclear war and its terrible aftermath, he cannot bear to look at her (p. 132). In this part she acts as a critic and a prophet, telling Simon that the future does not lie with the 'dinosaurs in a bunker' but with Lilith and Laura, the mutants. Look carefully at what Catherine says in this part. Does it tell us anything about the character of Catherine or is the author using her to suggest alternatives for the future? Catherine often acts as a functionary in that she fills in the gaps between sections, offering information which we would not otherwise receive and suggesting possible future values.

## DWIGHT ALLISON

Dwight is the son of Colonel Allison and the brother of Wayne who finally marries Ophelia. He appears in the flesh only in Part 2 as a rebel against General MacAllister's organisation though there are several significant references to him in Part 3. Ophelia is obviously attracted to him although she does not necessarily agree with his ideas. He has listened to Bill's teaching and has acted upon it. A fiery, challenging character, he can be seen as either hot-headed or a man of action. Look carefully at his arguments and his actions and see what effect he has. His direct action helps the survivors keep their cows – which might be seen as saving the settlement – when Colonel Allison comes to requisition them, and in Part 3 we hear that he built the Abbey at Timperley. It is this that convinces Simon that he, too, could play a part in the future.

*A boy of action and of spirit*

## OPHELIA

*Weaker in character than her sisters*

*Torn between her loves and her fear*

*Significance of the name.*

*Conflicts for Ophelia between her love for Dwight and her father and her need for security.*

*Is Ophelia as strong as her sisters?*

It is interesting that Bill Harnden names his daughter after the character in Shakespeare's *Hamlet*, a book given to him by Veronica, which he had in his briefcase on the day of the explosion. When she is born, Bill quotes Hamlet himself, 'Let her not walk i' the sun' (p. 69), words which refer to Ophelia, Polonius's daughter in the play. The warning has a double meaning. It could simply mean that the girl should not walk in the sun and get sunburnt, which in Elizabethan days was not acceptable for women of high rank. Obviously this meaning has a deeper relevance to 'outside' after the nuclear war when the sun's rays have become dangerous because of the damage to the atmosphere. Another meaning is linked to the pun on 'sun'. Remembering that audiences hear rather than read words, the obvious second meaning is not to let Ophelia get too close to the 'son', i.e. to Hamlet himself. Apart from the sexual implications it could be a warning that those too close to power will fall with it, as of course Ophelia in *Hamlet* does. Bill would have known all these meanings. With hindsight the warning may also relate to her friendship with Dwight Allison who rebels against his father's military organisation although of course Bill did not know this when Ophelia was born.

Ophelia finds herself in a difficult position in the bunker. She understands her mother's, Erica Kowlanski's attitude and views but she loves her father to whom she is close. There are times when she does not seem to understand fully what Bill is trying to do but follows him because she loves him.

As they share the same father, it might be interesting to compare Ophelia with Sarah and Catherine. You might like to compare her journey outside to warn the survivors with Sarah's journeys, first to get supplies, and then to take Catherine to Johnson. The author tells us that 'Ophelia did not much care who was right or wrong' (p. 70). She does not appear to have a sense of purpose, unlike her sisters who both understood the importance of survival, and seems reluctant to become involved in issues.

*Would you agree that Ophelia is a weak character?*

You may wish to ask yourself how much sympathy you have for her. Think about how she compares with Dwight Allison and his actions. Do you think that having Erica for her mother explains the differences?

## SIMON

Simon is the son of Ophelia and Wayne Allison and although his age is not mentioned, he appears slightly older than Laura who is probably around eighteen. He discovers that his uncle Dwight built the Abbey at Timperley and that Laura's mother was his aunt. Although Part 3 is indirectly told through Simon's eyes, the reader can see the conflict going on inside him. Look at how he sees Laura when he first meets her and the problems he has with her 'superior' knowledge and skills. He realises that his people are 'dinosaurs in a bunker' (p. 121) and feels useless, as Bill did when he joined the bunker. Part 3 is a period of growth for Simon; a development stage.

**Forced to face reality**
**Not insensitive**
**Frightened and angry**
*Look at how Simon's feelings, views and attitudes change.*

By focusing on how Simon feels, the author helps the reader to understand what it must be like to be 'outside'. Simon struggles with his feelings about himself and Laura. He wants to feel superior and normal, but Laura's abilities remind him all the time that he cannot cope with the new world without her help. You might like to think about whether Simon would have reacted in the same way had he been a girl.

He seems prejudiced against Laura's appearance but this may be because he is frightened of her, as his mother was frightened of Lilith. You may wish to think

*Is Simon proud?*

about this. He finally comes to understand both Laura and himself. Once he can find a place for himself in the future, his attitude changes.

## LAURA

*A mutant
Gentle
Generous
Sensitive
Intelligent*

*How do we learn
about Laura?*

*The new
humanity*

Laura represents the future human being, the product of a society based on the principles of cooperation, formulated by Johnson and Catherine, a society which has developed genetically to cope with the new environment. Her psychic skills represent insight and she uses them to good effect.

The reader is not really given her point of view except through the eyes of Simon who observes her behaviour and hears what she says to him. We never see her out of Simon's company. When she is first introduced, she is not described before she speaks, 'Weapons are evil!' (p. 120). She sounds almost biblical in her description of the holocaust, and she is a pacifist, 'You have no right to destroy any living thing!' (p. 120). Simon cannot understand this as he believes that by shooting the dog he saved her life. He has yet to learn that she can control the minds of living things and has no need of his gun.

When Laura is described, we learn only about her clothing – the exterior of the person which indicates that Simon (and perhaps by implication the reader) is not looking in sufficient depth to see the real person. The craftsmanship that went into the making of her clothes is symbolic of society's return to the natural and the rediscovery of the spiritual. The use of moccasins and beads suggests societies which were reputed to be peaceful until they were finally destroyed by technology and guns.

Simon describes Laura's eyes first (p. 121). Eyes are usually significant in literature because they are seen as symbols of the inner self. Laura is not blind as Simon originally thought but has mutated eyes: 'Black pin-prick pupils looked at him and saw, and he could feel her pity'. Laura's empathy and pity offend Simon most. Throughout this part of the novel, Laura endeavours to understand Simon, despite the fact that he appears to make no attempt to understand her. This is typical of Laura's society; Catherine still has feelings of anger and contempt towards Simon, but Laura continually forgives and is gentle despite her psychic powers. She does not respond to his aggression, rudeness and dismissal with anything but sympathy and an attempt to understand him. Ironically this makes the situation worse for him.

*Does the description of Laura repel you?*

When he notices the fine hair that covers Laura's body he describes her as a 'throw-back! A congenital ape!' (p. 122). Simon's treatment of her continues to be ungrateful and aggressive and yet she still helps him throughout this part of the novel. She outlines some of her philosophy in the taking of the jewels from the dead. She explains that the dead have no use for them and neither does she, therefore giving them to the artisans (who do have a use for them) is the most logical thing. She gives without expecting anything back in return. This underpins her relationship with Simon. She gives him as much as she can and does not seem to expect anything in return. Because Simon has been brought up in a different culture, he cannot understand this and resents her all the more for it.

**The holocaust as a rebirth**

We learn that Laura views the holocaust as a new beginning rather than an end (p. 127). The link with God and Christianity becomes clear – her society is not a pagan one. This philosophy underlies the way she sees the present world as better than the one which was destroyed and her new species as an improved version of the society that gave birth to Simon. Because she is so gentle, generous and resourceful, the reader is encouraged to agree with her rather than think her arrogant.

It is important that the reader sees Laura as a representative of the new society rather than as a saintly, exceptional individual, and the responses of other members of the community to Simon's presence are given to show that they too share her philosophy (p. 137).

## BILL HARNDEN

*Sensitive, artistic and humane*
*Concerned about the future*
*Influential on young people*

Bill is briefly mentioned in Part 1 as the absent father teaching English literature at Bristol University. He is more important in Part 2 as the inspiration for Dwight Allison to challenge the authority of the military in the bunker. Much of Part 2 is told from his point of view and encourages the reader to think about whether MacAllister is right about the way he organises the survivors.

*What is the link between Bill's ideas and Catherine's?*

In the bunker Bill realises that his knowledge and skills are considered useless, and the idea that technology, science and 'ranking' are vital is challenged through his views (pp. 66–7). He appears to be alone in thinking this until his student, Dwight Allison, takes up his beliefs and acts upon them.

*How influential has Bill been on the future?*

After he has met his daughter Catherine and brought Dwight to the settlement to warn them of Colonel Allison's 'raid', he returns to the bunker to live to nearly ninety. You may wish to consider whether he had any influence on his grandson, Simon, and if so, whether this finally helped Simon understand his role in the future.

*What purpose does Bill have?*

Because we gain so much knowledge of how Bill feels, he is more of a personality, and his character can be studied closely.

## LILITH

*The first of the mutants*
*All-seeing*
*Possessing paranormal powers*

Lilith, Catherine's first surviving child and Bill's granddaughter, is obviously unusual. You may wish to think about the significance of her name. In some versions of the Bible, Lilith was the first wife of Adam in the Old Testament and referred to as 'screech owl' (Authorised Version, Isaiah 34:14) and 'night monster' (Revised Version). In Babylonian mythology, she was said to haunt wilderness in storms and was believed to be dangerous to children. You may wish to think about this especially as Lilith disposes of deformed babies who are unlikely to live. We first hear about her from Catherine who describes her as her only surviving child out of seven. Catherine says, 'I've Lilith to help me' (p. 103) and 'I think she sees too much, but Johnson says we have to heed her, however hard it seems' (p. 104). We also see her from Ophelia's viewpoint as the murderess of her own mother's children

*How do you feel about Lilith through this section?*

(p. 107). When Ophelia meets Lilith (p. 104), she assumes that Lilith is blind until she realises that Lilith is not blind at all, that in fact she 'could see everything' (p. 105).

Lilith is the first of the new human beings, the ones who have mutated to cope with the new environment; and she has developed paranormal powers. To begin with she is described as a skinny flaxen-haired girl in a plain grey dress (p. 104). Only later (p. 108) is she seen

*Why do you think the author presents Lilith through Ophelia?*

as a horror, again through Ophelia's eyes. When her appearance is described in full (p. 108) – hair so fair as to be almost white, pale down on her face and arms almost like fur, white eyes with pin-prick black pupils – it is not exactly a picture of horror even if it is strange.

*What impact does*
*Lilith have at the*
*end of this section?*

Ophelia is, no doubt, frightened of Lilith, just as Simon is in Part 3. It is her laugh that scares them and her pity for them that disturbs them. Her pitying smile closes Part 2 (p. 114).

You might like to compare Lilith's physical appearance to Laura's. Both are mutants, and are only one generation apart (Lilith is Laura's aunt). Yet while Simon comes to see Laura as beautiful he continues to be repelled and frightened by Lilith. Was the author's intention perhaps to point to the evolution of the mutants here?

# LANGUAGE & STYLE

## NARRATION

The story is told by a narrator who is not a **character** (see Literary Terms) in the novel. This **third person narrative** (see Literary Terms) allows the author to show the reader events, feelings and attitudes that might not be known to a narrator who is a character in the story (**first person narrative** – see Literary Terms). It enables the readers to gain knowledge of any character's feelings. However, each of the three parts of the novel is told from the point of view of the character whose name is the title of the part. In Part 1, although we are told by the narrator how Veronica feels and sees, most of the action is seen through Sarah's eyes. This narrative technique enables the author to create suspense as we can never be sure what will happen to the characters in the course of the story. If one character tells the story then we know that that character must have survived in order to recollect the events.

Third person narrative closely connected with a character also gives us the opportunity to share in the feelings and perceptions of this central character whilst giving us enough distance to be critical of the character's views. This is particularly important when we think of how Ophelia and Simon initially feel about Catherine's (blind Kate's) community. This style of 'telling' is also called **indirect discourse** (see Literary Terms).

## SETTING

*Role of the setting*

The author uses the environment to suggest positive and negative aspects of the events described. In Part 1, she gives something abstract, such as darkness, which is not alive, the ability to 'howl', and wind screams as if it were alive. This device is called **personification** (see Literary Terms), and it makes the environment almost a living creature with motives and intentions. She uses this device in **similes** (see Literary Terms) such as 'darkness that smashed like a gigantic fist against the house' (p. 15). The effect is to stress the vulnerability of the family inside the house. The device also suggests that the environment is against their survival, intending to destroy them, which of course it is. The author also describes the environment to show that the destruction which takes place is caused by people, not by natural disaster.

In literature, the weather and environment are often used to reflect mood, tone and to indicate whether or not something good or bad is going to happen. This is called **pathetic fallacy** (see Literary Terms). In this novel the reverse of pathetic fallacy is used. Parts 1 and 2 both open with descriptions of an idyllic summer day with nature at peace at the very moment when the explosion takes place. This contrast of the environment with a nuclear destruction separates the natural world from the man-made disaster that is about to happen.

## IMAGERY

*Imagery used to spell out a message.*

Equally the gorse flower at the end of Part 1 indicates a promise of hope in the future, in contrast with the ghoulish shapes in the churchyard (p. 54). What humanity has done to the environment is described throughout the three parts, and the **imagery** (see Literary Terms) of the natural world is employed to stress that hope for the future lies in people turning back to nature.

In Part 2, for instance, the description of the Gloucester area outside the bunker (p. 91) suggests that what had been made by technology has been destroyed, or broken by its own decay. In contrast, when we move away from the bunker towards Catherine's and Johnson's settlement, we find descriptions of new life and new hope.

All through the story the author uses descriptions of the environment to demonstrate who is to blame for the disaster and to show how nature will survive and prove stronger than the technology that made the bombs. Careful reading of this text will reveal the frequent use of imagery to create the desired effect.

## BIBLICAL REFERENCES

There are several people in the story named after biblical characters, and there is a parallel drawn between the holocaust of nuclear war and the various biblical purges by flood, fire and plague. There is an obvious link with Noah's flood and the destruction of the cities of Sodom and Gomorrah. Catherine's dream in Part 1 of remaking the Garden of Eden appears to come true in Part 3, and there is a suggestion that the nuclear war acted as a purging of the old ways which are still followed by the bunker people who are becoming extinct in Part 3. As Part 1 develops, Sarah begins to understand the role of a nondenominational God in comforting the dying, and the part concludes with hope for the future in the description of the gorse flower. In contrast, the bunker society is almost godless in its worship of technology and science.

Laura's condemnation of weapons sounds almost like the words of an Old Testament preacher – her tone is particularly strident, reinforcing the idea of ridding the world of evil (p. 119).

## PRESENTATION OF POINTS OF VIEW

Louise Lawrence has said that her novel was criticised for 'advocating nuclear war' (presumably as a way of purging mankind of evil), an idea which she strongly denies. The author certainly seems to approve more of Johnson's and Catherine's ideas than of those of MacAllister, concerning the organisation of post-holocaust society. You may wish to read the narrative carefully looking at how she presents the different organisations. Obviously, the incident with the cattle and the sympathy we have for Dwight will suggest to us that the bunker people are wrong. It is very difficult for us to criticise Johnson and Catherine who give what they have to others to help their survival, and equally it is hard for us to agree with MacAllister who effectively steals what he wants. Although Part 3 is told from Simon's viewpoint, we recognise that he is being unfair in his treatment of Laura who is helping him. It is through descriptions of their various points of view that the author conveys an opinion with which the reader is encouraged to agree. If she is not impartial in her descriptions, the matters that she is discussing are perhaps not of a kind that would permit impartiality.

# PART FOUR

# STUDY SKILLS

## HOW TO USE QUOTATIONS

One of the secrets of success in writing essays is the way you use quotations. There are five basic principles:

- Put inverted commas at the beginning and end of the quotation
- Write the quotation exactly as it appears in the original
- Do not use a quotation that repeats what you have just written
- Use the quotation so that it fits into your sentence
- Keep the quotation as short as possible

Quotations should be used to develop the line of thought in your essays.

Your comment should not duplicate what is in your quotation. For example:

> Bill Harnden was not happy in the Avon bunker. 'Bill Harnden continued his life in the Avon bunker, but he was not entirely happy with the situation.'

Far more effective is to write:

> The author tells us that 'Bill Harnden continued his life in the Avon bunker, but he was not entirely happy with the situation'.

However, the most sophisticated way of using the writer's words is to embed them into your sentence:

> Although Bill Harnden remained in the Avon bunker he was not 'entirely happy with the situation'.

When you use quotations in this way, you are demonstrating the ability to use text as evidence to support your ideas - not simply including words from the original to prove you have read it.

Everyone writes differently. Work through the suggestions given here and adapt the advice to suit your own style and interests. This will improve your essay-writing skills and allow your personal voice to emerge.

The following points indicate in ascending order the skills of essay writing:

- Picking out one or two facts about the story and adding the odd detail
- Writing about the text by retelling the story
- Retelling the story and adding a quotation here and there
- Organising an answer which explains what is happening in the text and giving quotations to support what you write

....................................................................

- Writing in such a way as to show that you have thought about the intentions of the writer of the text and that you understand the techniques used
- Writing at some length, giving your viewpoint on the text and commenting by picking out details to support your views
- Looking at the text as a work of art, demonstrating clear critical judgement and explaining to the reader of your essay how the enjoyment of the text is assisted by literary devices, linguistic effects and psychological insights; showing how the text relates to the time when it was written

The dotted line above represents the division between lower- and higher-level grades. Higher-level performance begins when you start to consider your response as a reader of the text. The highest level is reached when you offer an enthusiastic personal response and show how this piece of literature is a product of its time.

*Coursework*
*essay*

Set aside an hour or so at the start of your work to plan what you have to do.

- List all the points you feel are needed to cover the task. Collect page references of information and quotations that will support what you have to say. A helpful tool is the highlighter pen: this saves painstaking copying and enables you to target precisely what you want to use.
- Focus on what you consider to be the main points of the essay. Try to sum up your argument in a single sentence, which could be the closing sentence of your essay. Depending on the essay title, it could be a statement about a character: Catherine and Johnson share their abhorrence of violence of any kind and their fierce hope for the revival of life and the growth of a new, better society; an opinion about setting: The settlement that grew up round Johnson's nursery garden is a symbol of the gradual fulfilment of mankind's hopes for survival and regeneration; or a judgement on a theme: Survival through adaptation and evolution is perhaps the most important theme in the novel, offering hope for a new life growing out of desolation.
- Make a short essay plan. Use the first paragraph to introduce the argument you wish to make. In the following paragraphs develop this argument with details, examples and other possible points of view. Sum up your argument in the last paragraph. Check you have answered the question.
- Write the essay, remembering all the time the central point you are making.
- On completion, go back over what you have written to eliminate careless errors and improve expression. Read it aloud to yourself, or, if you are feeling more confident, to a relative or friend.

*Examination* If you can, try to type your essay, using a word
*essay* processor. This will allow you to correct and improve
your writing without spoiling its appearance.

The essay written in an examination often carries more
marks than the coursework essay even though it is
written under considerable time pressure.

In the revision period build up notes on various aspects
of the text you are using. Fortunately, in acquiring this
set of York Notes on *Children of the Dust*, you have
made a prudent beginning! York Notes are set out to
give you vital information and help you to construct
your personal overview of the text.

Make notes with appropriate quotations about the key
issues of the set text. Go into the examination knowing
your text and having a clear set of opinions about it.

In most English Literature examinations you can take
in copies of your set books. This in an enormous
advantage although it may lull you into a false sense of
security. Beware! There is simply not enough time in an
examination to read the book from scratch.

*In the* • Read the question paper carefully and remind
*examination*   yourself what you have to do.
• Look at the questions on your set texts to select the
  one that most interests you and mentally work out
  the points you wish to stress.
• Remind yourself of the time available and how you
  are going to use it.
• Briefly map out a short plan in note form that will
  keep your writing on track and illustrate the key
  argument you want to make.
• Then set about writing it.
• When you have finished, check through to eliminate
  errors.

*To summarise,*
*these are keys*
*to success*

- Know the text
- Have a clear understanding of and opinions on the storyline, characters, setting, themes and writer's concerns
- Select the right material
- Plan and write a clear response, continually bearing the question in mind

# SAMPLE ESSAY PLAN

A typical essay question on *Children of the Dust* is followed by a sample essay plan in note form. This does not present the only answer to the question, merely one possible answer out of several. Do not be afraid to include your own ideas, and leave out some of those in the sample! Remember that quotations are essential to prove and illustrate the points you make.

**Discuss the role of conflict in *Children of the Dust*. How is it successfully resolved?**

This question is in two parts and you need to address both of them equally. It is better to consider them together when planning your essay rather than deal with them separately.

*Introduction*

The outbreak of nuclear war, the result of international conflict, is the context of the book and starts everything that follows. There are different sorts of conflict considered in the book: family conflict, political conflict and personal conflict. Laura's community in Part 3 offers a model of living that has resolved most destructive conflicts.

*Part 1:*
*Family*
*conflict*

- Conflict between Veronica and Sarah; look at how and why this is resolved
- Conflict between Veronica and the younger children shows parent-child conflict; examine how and why it occurs; how is it resolved?
- Conflict of need. Family members need different things for different reasons. Look at this carefully

*Part 2:*
*Political*
*conflict*

- Examine the different opinions on policy priorities and political organisation
- Dwight Allison resists and rebels; examine why and how
- Bill's views and why they may differ from MacAllister's opinions
- Dwight's 'direct action' of warning the survivors sets up a conflict with his father over politics
- The confrontations between differing views and the results of these

*Part 3:*
*Personal*
*conflict*

- Ophelia's inner conflict between her loyalty to her father and to Dwight, and her conformist nature and preference for the bunker
- Conflict within Simon and how he resolves this

*Conclusion*

List the main points of the various conflicts and show how harmony can finally be restored.

# FURTHER QUESTIONS

1 Strength of character and strength of purpose seem to be important issues in *Children of the Dust*. Select one or two characters from the book and discuss how far this is true of them.
2 Louise Lawrence said that she hoped to 'touch every young person who read [*Children of the Dust*] by the potential horror', in order that they would change the future which was threatened by nuclear war. How far do you think she has been successful in 'touching' you with her novel?
3 The topic of nuclear war is always depressing. How has Louise Lawrence made her story optimistic?
4 At the end of the novel, Simon does not begrudge Laura or 'any of them' the knowledge he possesses. Discuss what Simon has learned during Part 3 and how he came to understand.

5 Discuss the role of Dwight Allison in both Parts 2 and 3. How far do you think he represents the 'young person' the author wishes to touch and change?

6 Ophelia appears to be the weakest of Bill Harnden's family. How far would you agree with this view of her and why?

7 Discuss how Louise Lawrence uses descriptions of the environment to emphasise the message of *Children of the Dust*.

8 Describe the different forms of organisation outlined in *Children of the Dust* and examine how the author shows the reader which form she regards as preferable for the future.

9 'Dinosaurs in a bunker' is a theme which recurs in both Parts 2 and 3. How important do you think this is as a theme of the novel, and how has the author explored it?

10 Discuss the lesson Simon learns in Part 3. How far do you sympathise with him?

11 One optimistic point of the novel is the possibility of human survival in the face of world destruction. Examine the ways used by the author to convey this. You should look at:
   • symbols using natural environment
   • development of the human race
   • learning and understanding

12 Do you consider Bill Harnden a significant character in *Children of the Dust*?

13 The novel often places the natural environment and human technology in conflict with each other. Examine how the author deals with this and comment on the outcome.

14 How effective do you find the division of the book into three parts? Comment on what is achieved by this technique.

# PART FIVE

# CULTURAL CONNECTIONS

## BROADER PERSPECTIVES

*Nuclear war in literature*

With the threat of nuclear war dominating the fifties and sixties, there are many books that explore what would happen if a nuclear war occurred. One of the earliest is *On The Beach* by Nevil Shute (Heinemann, 1957; paperback, Mandarin, 1990) which focuses on men in a submarine, separated from their families who are already possibly dead, and how they cope with their predicament. Several books fit well with *Children of the Dust,* including *A Rag, A Bone and A Hank of Hair* by Nicholas Fisk (Kestrel, 1980; paperback, Puffin, 1982), which shows anarchy and the breakdown of community. *Z for Zachariah* by R.C. O'Brien (Heinemann Educational, 1973) shows how difficult people find living together, even when the two of them may be the only people left alive.

*Post-apocalyptic novels and films*

Although it is useful to understand the Cold War and the nuclear threat, this book is best understood in the context of the post-apocalyptic novel. Exploring how survivors would cope and develop society when mass destruction has taken place is a theme common with popular science fiction. One of the earliest books in this genre is *The War of the Worlds* by H.G. Wells (1898). John Wyndham has written several books on the theme of civilisation threatened by alien invasion, epidemic diseases or warfare. The films *Blade Runner* (1982, directed by Ridley Scott) and *Mad Max* (1972, directed by George Miller) both explore the breakdown of civilisation and offer the pessimistic view that control would return to the strongest and most ruthless. Other works offer a more positive view.

**character** invented, imaginary person in a work of fiction or a play

**first person narrative** story told in the first person singular by a person who is a character in the story (sometimes called the 'I' narrator)

**image** a word-picture which appeals to the senses, to the imagination

**imagery** figurative language in a piece of literature, that is, all the words in such a work which refer to objects and qualities which appeal to the senses and the feelings, to the reader's imagination

**indirect discourse** story told exclusively from the viewpoint of one of the characters in a story who is not the narrator

**pathetic fallacy** assumption that the natural world shares the writer's mood: weather is gloomy because the writer is sad

**personification** form of poetic language in which things or ideas are treated as if they were human, and given human characteristics and feelings

**simile** a very common figure of speech in which one thing is said to be like another. A simile always contains the word 'as' or 'like'

**structure** organisation of a literary work to create a meaningful pattern

**style** characteristic manner in which a writer expresses himself or herself; the particular manner of any literary work

**theme** central idea of a work of literature, either directly stated or implied indirectly. A text may contain several themes

**third person narrative** story told by a narrator (usually anonymous) who is not a character in the story

# TEST ANSWERS

**TEST YOURSELF (Part 1)**

A
•••
1 Sarah
2 Veronica
3 William
4 Veronica
5 Veronica
6 Buster the dog
7 Catherine

**TEST YOURSELF (Part 2)**

A
•••
1 Erica
2 Bill
3 Ophelia

4 Dwight
5 Johnson
6 Erica
7 Lilith

**TEST YOURSELF (Part 3)**

A
•••
1 Laura
2 Catherine (Blind Kate)
3 Laura
4 Catherine (Blind Kate)
5 Simon
6 The bunker people
7 Simon

# NOTES

# Notes

# NOTES

# NOTES

# NOTES

## GCSE and equivalent levels (£3.50 each)

Maya Angelou
*I Know Why the Caged Bird Sings*

Jane Austen
*Pride and Prejudice*

Harold Brighouse
*Hobson's Choice*

Charlotte Brontë
*Jane Eyre*

Emily Brontë
*Wuthering Heights*

Charles Dickens
*David Copperfield*

Charles Dickens
*Great Expectations*

Charles Dickens
*Hard Times*

George Eliot
*Silas Marner*

William Golding
*Lord of the Flies*

Willis Hall
*The Long and the Short and the Tall*

Thomas Hardy
*Far from the Madding Crowd*

Thomas Hardy
*The Mayor of Casterbridge*

Thomas Hardy
*Tess of the d'Urbervilles*

L.P. Hartley
*The Go-Between*

Seamus Heaney
*Selected Poems*

Susan Hill
*I'm the King of the Castle*

Barry Hines
*A Kestrel for a Knave*

Louise Lawrence
*Children of the Dust*

Harper Lee
*To Kill a Mockingbird*

Laurie Lee
*Cider with Rosie*

Arthur Miller
*A View from the Bridge*

Arthur Miller
*The Crucible*

Robert O'Brien
*Z for Zachariah*

George Orwell
*Animal Farm*

J.B. Priestley
*An Inspector Calls*

Willy Russell
*Educating Rita*

Willy Russell
*Our Day Out*

J.D. Salinger
*The Catcher in the Rye*

William Shakespeare
*Henry V*

William Shakespeare
*Julius Caesar*

William Shakespeare
*Macbeth*

William Shakespeare
*A Midsummer Night's Dream*

William Shakespeare
*The Merchant of Venice*

William Shakespeare
*Romeo and Juliet*

William Shakespeare
*The Tempest*

William Shakespeare
*Twelfth Night*

George Bernard Shaw
*Pygmalion*

R.C. Sherriff
*Journey's End*

Rukshana Smith
*Salt on the snow*

John Steinbeck
*Of Mice and Men*

R.L. Stevenson
*Dr Jekyll and Mr Hyde*

Robert Swindells
*Daz 4 Zoe*

Mildred D. Taylor
*Roll of Thunder, Hear My Cry*

Mark Twain
*The Adventures of Huckleberry Finn*

James Watson
*Talking in Whispers*

*A Choice of Poets*

*Nineteenth Century Short Stories*

*Poetry of the First World War*

*Six Women Poets*

## Advanced level (£3.99 each)

Margaret Atwood
*The Handmaid's Tale*

William Blake
*Songs of Innocence and of Experience*

Emily Brontë
*Wuthering Heights*

Geoffrey Chaucer
*The Wife of Bath's Prologue and Tale*

Joseph Conrad
*Heart of Darkness*

Charles Dickens
*Great Expectations*

F. Scott Fitzgerald
*The Great Gatsby*

Thomas Hardy
*Tess of the d'Urbervilles*

James Joyce
*Dubliners*

Arthur Miller
*Death of a Salesman*

William Shakespeare
*Antony and Cleopatra*

William Shakespeare
*Hamlet*

William Shakespeare
*King Lear*

William Shakespeare
*The Merchant of Venice*

William Shakespeare
*Romeo and Juliet*

William Shakespeare
*The Tempest*

Mary Shelley
*Frankenstein*

Alice Walker
*The Color Purple*

Tennessee Williams
*A Streetcar Named Desire*

Jane Austen
*Emma*

Jane Austen
*Pride and Prejudice*

Charlotte Brontë
*Jane Eyre*

Seamus Heaney
*Selected Poems*

William Shakespeare
*Much Ado About Nothing*

William Shakespeare
*Othello*

John Webster
*The Duchess of Malfi*

Chinua Achebe
*Things Fall Apart*

Edward Albee
*Who's Afraid of Virginia Woolf?*

Jane Austen
*Mansfield Park*

Jane Austen
*Northanger Abbey*

Jane Austen
*Persuasion*

Jane Austen
*Sense and Sensibility*

Samuel Beckett
*Waiting for Godot*

Alan Bennett
*Talking Heads*

John Betjeman
*Selected Poems*

Robert Bolt
*A Man for All Seasons*

Robert Burns
*Selected Poems*

Lord Byron
*Selected Poems*

Geoffrey Chaucer
*The Franklin's Tale*

Geoffrey Chaucer
*The Merchant's Tale*

Geoffrey Chaucer
*The Miller's Tale*

Geoffrey Chaucer
*The Nun's Priest's Tale*

Geoffrey Chaucer
*Prologue to the Canterbury Tales*

Samuel Taylor Coleridge
*Selected Poems*

Daniel Defoe
*Moll Flanders*

Daniel Defoe
*Robinson Crusoe*

Shelagh Delaney
*A Taste of Honey*

Charles Dickens
*Bleak House*

Charles Dickens
*Oliver Twist*

Emily Dickinson
*Selected Poems*

John Donne
*Selected Poems*

Douglas Dunn
*Selected Poems*

George Eliot
*Middlemarch*

George Eliot
*The Mill on the Floss*

T.S. Eliot
*The Waste Land*

T.S. Eliot
*Selected Poems*

Henry Fielding
*Joseph Andrews*

E.M. Forster
*Howards End*

E.M. Forster
*A Passage to India*

John Fowles
*The French Lieutenant's Woman*

Brian Friel
*Translations*

Elizabeth Gaskell
*North and South*

Oliver Goldsmith
*She Stoops to Conquer*

Graham Greene
*Brighton Rock*

Thomas Hardy
*Jude the Obscure*

Thomas Hardy
*Selected Poems*

Nathaniel Hawthorne
*The Scarlet Letter*

Ernest Hemingway
*The Old Man and the Sea*

Homer
*The Iliad*

Homer
*The Odyssey*

Aldous Huxley
*Brave New World*

Ben Jonson
*The Alchemist*

Ben Jonson
*Volpone*

James Joyce
*A Portrait of the Artist as a Young Man*

John Keats
*Selected Poems*

Philip Larkin
*Selected Poems*

D.H. Lawrence
*The Rainbow*

D.H. Lawrence
*Sons and Lovers*

D.H. Lawrence
*Women in Love*

Christopher Marlowe
*Doctor Faustus*

John Milton
*Paradise Lost Bks I & II*

John Milton
*Paradise Lost IV & IX*

Sean O'Casey
*Juno and the Paycock*

George Orwell
*Nineteen Eighty-four*

John Osborne
*Look Back in Anger*

Wilfred Owen
*Selected Poems*

Harold Pinter
*The Caretaker*

Sylvia Plath
*Selected Works*

Alexander Pope
*Selected Poems*

Jean Rhys
*Wide Sargasso Sea*

William Shakespeare
*As You Like It*

William Shakespeare
*Coriolanus*

William Shakespeare
*Henry IV Pt 1*

William Shakespeare
*Henry V*

William Shakespeare
*Julius Caesar*

William Shakespeare
*Measure for Measure*

William Shakespeare
*Much Ado About Nothing*

William Shakespeare
*A Midsummer Night's Dream*

William Shakespeare
*Richard II*

William Shakespeare
*Richard III*

William Shakespeare
*Sonnets*

William Shakespeare
*The Taming of the Shrew*

William Shakespeare
*The Winter's Tale*

George Bernard Shaw
*Arms and the Man*

George Bernard Shaw
*Saint Joan*

Richard Brinsley Sheridan
*The Rivals*

Muriel Spark
*The Prime of Miss Jean Brodie*

John Steinbeck
*The Grapes of Wrath*

John Steinbeck
*The Pearl*

Tom Stoppard
*Rosencrantz and Guildenstern are Dead*

Jonathan Swift
*Gulliver's Travels*

John Millington Synge
*The Playboy of the Western World*

W.M. Thackeray
*Vanity Fair*

Virgil
*The Aeneid*

Derek Walcott
*Selected Poems*

Oscar Wilde
*The Importance of Being Earnest*

Tennessee Williams
*Cat on a Hot Tin Roof*

Tennessee Williams
*The Glass Menagerie*

Virginia Woolf
*Mrs Dalloway*

Virginia Woolf
*To the Lighthouse*

William Wordsworth
*Selected Poems*

W.B. Yeats
*Selected Poems*

# York Notes – the Ultimate Literature Guides

York Notes are recognised as the best literature study guides.
If you have enjoyed using this book and have found it useful, you
can now order others directly from us – simply follow the ordering
instructions below.

## HOW TO ORDER

Decide which title(s) you require and then order in one of the following
ways:

**Booksellers**
All titles available from good bookstores.

**By post**
List the title(s) you require in the space provided overleaf,
select your method of payment, complete your name and
address details and return your completed order form and
payment to:

*Addison Wesley Longman Ltd*
*PO BOX 88*
*Harlow*
*Essex CM19 5SR*

**By phone**
Call our Customer Information Centre on 01279 623923 to
place your order, quoting mail number: HEYN1.

**By fax**
Complete the order form overleaf, ensuring you fill in your
name and address details and method of payment, and fax it
to us on 01279 414130.

**By e-mail**
E-mail your order to us on awlhe.orders@awl.co.uk listing
title(s) and quantity required and providing full name and
address details as requested overleaf. Please quote mail
number: HEYN1. Please do not send credit card details by
e-mail.

# York Notes Order Form

## Titles required:

| Quantity | Title/ISBN | Price |
|----------|-----------|-------|
|          |           |       |
|          |           |       |
|          |           |       |
|          |           |       |
|          |           |       |
|          |           |       |

Sub total _____

Please add £2.50 postage & packing _____

*(P & P is free for orders over £50)* _____

**Total** _____

Mail no: HEYN1

Your Name _____

Your Address _____

Postcode _____ Telephone _____

## Method of payment

☐ I enclose a cheque or a P/O for £_____ made payable to Addison Wesley Longman Ltd

☐ Please charge my Visa/Access/AMEX/Diners Club card
Number _____ Expiry Date _____
Signature _____ Date _____

*(please ensure that the address given above is the same as for your credit card)*

*Prices and other details are correct at time of going to press but may change without notice. All orders are subject to status.*

☐ *Please tick this box if you would like a complete listing of Longman Study Guides (suitable for GCSE and A-level students)*

York Press

Longman

Addison
Wesley
Longman